CAREERS IN THE
BUILDING TRADES

A GROWING DEMAND

Roofer

Careers in the Building Trades

A Growing Demand

 Apprenticeships

 Carpenter

Construction & Building Inspector

 Electrician

 Flooring Installer

Heating and Cooling Technician

Masonry Worker

 Plumber

 Roofer

Working in Green Construction

CAREERS IN THE
BUILDING TRADES

A GROWING DEMAND

Roofer

Andrew Morkes

MASON CREST

Mason Crest
450 Parkway Drive, Suite D
Broomall, Pennsylvania 19008
(866) MCP-BOOK (toll-free)
www.masoncrest.com

First printing

9 8 7 6 5 4 3 2 1

ISBN (hardback) 978-1-4222-4119-6

ISBN (series) 978-1-4222-4110-3

ISBN (ebook) 978-1-4222-7689-1

Cataloging-in-Publication Data on file with the Library of Congress

NATIONAL
HIGHLIGHTS

Developed and Produced by National Highlights Inc.
Proofreader: Mika Jin
Interior and cover design: Yolanda Van Cooten
Production: Michelle Luke

CONTENTS

KEY ICONS TO LOOK FOR:

Words to understand: These words with their easy-to-understand definitions will increase the reader's understanding of the text while building vocabulary skills.

Sidebars: This boxed material within the main text allows readers to build knowledge, gain insights, explore possibilities, and broaden their perspectives by weaving together additional information to provide realistic and holistic perspectives.

Educational Videos: Readers can view videos by scanning our QR codes, providing them with additional educational content to supplement the text. Examples include news coverage, moments in history, speeches, iconic sports moments and much more!

Text-dependent questions: These questions send the reader back to the text for more careful attention to the evidence presented there.

Research projects: Readers are pointed toward areas of further inquiry connected to each chapter. Suggestions are provided for projects that encourage deeper research and analysis.

Series glossary of key terms: This back-of-the-book glossary contains terminology used throughout this series. Words found here increase the reader's ability to read and comprehend higher-level books and articles in this field.

INTRODUCTION

The Trades: Great Careers, Good Money, and Other Rewards

Trades workers play a major role in the success of economies throughout the world. They keep us cool in the summer and warm in the winter (heating and cooling technicians), build structures ranging from houses to skyscrapers (carpenters and ironworkers), and build and repair roofs that keep us protected from the elements (roofers), among many other job duties. Yet despite their important role in our society, only 6 percent of students consider a career in the trades, according to ExploretheTrades.org. Why? Because many young people have misconceptions about the trades. They have been told that the trades are low-paying, lack job security, and other untruths. In fact, working in the trades is one of the best career choices you can make. The following paragraphs provide more information on why a career in the trades is a good idea.

Good pay. Contrary to public perception, skilled trades workers earn salaries that place them firmly in the middle class. Average yearly salaries for construction workers (including those involved in the trades) in the United States are $48,900, according to the U.S. Department of Labor. This salary is slightly higher than the average earnings for some careers that require a bachelor's or graduate degree—including recreational therapists, $48,190; child, family, and school social workers, $47,510; and mental health counselors, $46,050. Trades workers who become managers or who launch their own businesses can have earnings that range from $90,000 to $200,000.

Strong employment prospects. There are shortages of trades workers throughout the world, according to the human resource consulting firm ManpowerGroup. In fact, trades workers are the most in-demand occupational field in the Americas, Europe, the Middle East, and Africa. They ranked fourth in the Asia-Pacific region.

Provides a comfortable life without a bachelor's or graduate degree. For decades in the United States and other countries, there has been an emphasis on earning a college degree as the key to life success. But studies show that only 35 percent of future jobs in the United States will require a four-year degree or higher. With college tuition continuing to increase and the chances of landing a good job out of college decreasing, a growing number of people are entering apprenticeship programs to prepare for careers in the trades. And unlike college students, apprentices receive a salary while learning and they don't have to pay off loans after they complete their education. It's a good feeling to start your career without $50,000 to $200,000 in college loans.

Rewarding work environment and many career options. A career in the trades is fulfilling because you get to use both your hands and your head to solve problems and make the world a better place. Many trades workers launch their own businesses.

Jobs can't be offshored. Trades careers involve hands-on work that requires the worker to be on-site to do his or her job. As a result, there is no chance that your position will be offshored to a foreign country. In an uncertain employment atmosphere, that's encouraging news.

Job opportunities are available throughout the United States and the world. There is a need for trades workers in small towns and big cities. If demand for their skills is not strong in their geographic area, they can move to other cities, states, or countries where demand is higher.

Are the Trades Right for Me?

Test your interest in the trades. How many of these statements do you agree with?

☐ **My favorite class in school is shop.**

☐ **I like to use power and hand tools.**

☐ **I enjoy observing work at construction sites.**

☐ **I like projects that allow me to work with my hands.**

☐ **I like to build and fix things.**

☐ **I like to watch home-repair shows on TV and the internet.**

☐ **I don't mind getting my hands dirty.**

☐ **I am good at math.**

☐ **I like to figure out how things work.**

If many of the statements above describe you, then you should consider a career in the trades. But you don't need to select a career right now. Check out this book on a career as a roofer and other books in the series to learn more about occupational paths in the trades. Good luck with your career exploration!

■ *Roofers not only construct the roofs of homes and stores, but also those of sports stadiums, such as the National Olympic Sports Complex Stadium in Kiev, Ukraine.*

Words to Understand

carcinogenic substances: Those known to cause cancer.

historical landmarks: Buildings or other structures that are protected under law because they have special value due to historical, cultural, or other factors.

photovoltaic: A type of technology that is used to generate electricity directly from sunlight via an electronic process.

solar energy: Energy that is produced by harvesting the heat and energy of the sun.

CHAPTER 1

What Do Roofers Do?

A roof is one of the basic needs of life. Without it (along with a house itself), we'd get wet in the rain, roasted by the summer sun, and covered in snow and hail. Life would be a mess without roofers, who repair old roofs and build new ones. Some roofers specialize in repairing or building roofs of business and commercial buildings, such as factories, sports stadiums, department stores, restaurants, and office buildings. Others focus on residential roof repair and construction. Still others focus on building and repairing green roofs or the roofs of historical landmarks or other structures. Roofers work for construction companies, small contractors, and government agencies. Others operate their own businesses.

Most aspiring roofers prepare for the field by completing on-the-job training. Others participate in apprenticeships or training programs at technical schools. Many cities, states, and countries require roofers to be licensed. Some roofers become certified to show customers that they have met the highest standards established by their industry.

■ *A career in roofing is a good choice for people who like to work outdoors.*

A career as a roofer is a physically demanding, but interesting, job. Many roofers like their jobs because every day is different, they get to work outdoors (some people might consider this a drawback), and they get to help build and repair structures that protect people from the elements.

■ *Learn more about the rewards of working as a roofer:*

What Roofers Do

The career of roofer may sound straightforward: you build roofs, right? But since roofs are an extremely important part of any structure, you need to know a lot to repair or build a quality roof. You need to know what type of roof works for a specific type of structure, what building techniques and materials to use, and much more. Here are some of the main duties of roofers on a repair job:

- Use digital tools and visual inspection methods to inspect roofs that are leaking or otherwise damaged to determine the best way to repair them
- Provide estimates to customers that detail the cost of repairs
- Erect scaffolding and ladders and rig safety equipment in preparation for the start of the job
- Replace damaged or missing shingles or tiles and damaged or rotting joists or plywood
- Replace or repair flashing around chimneys, walls, or vents
- Reapply waterproofing coatings to roofs or other surfaces

Roofers perform the following tasks when building a new roof:

- Measure roofs to calculate the quantities of materials needed
- Provide estimates to customers detailing the cost to replace a roof

The Types of Roofs

There are basically three types of roofs: flat, low-slope, and steep-slope roofs.

- **Flat roofs** are not perfectly flat; they typically have some elevation (height above a given level) to allow water to drain.
- A **low-slope roof** is one that rises up to three inches (0.0762 meters) per horizontal foot (or meter). They are typically used for apartment, commercial, and industrial buildings.
- A **steep-slope roof** is one that rises more than three inches (0.0762 meters) per horizontal foot (or meter). They are typically used for single-family homes.

- Set up scaffolding and ladders and rig safety equipment in preparation for the start of the job
- Tear off the existing roof and clean the roof deck in preparation for the installation of a new roof
- Install decking, which is often made of thick plywood
- Install plastic coatings, membranes, fiberglass, or felt over sloped roofs
- Install vapor barriers or layers of insulation on flat roofs
- Install ventilation systems such as turbine vents, gable or ridge vents, or exhaust fans
- Install shingles, asphalt, metal (steel, aluminum, etc.), wood, tiles, or other materials to make the roof weatherproof
- Cut and install flashing around chimneys, walls, or vents to prevent the entry of water
- Cover exposed nail or screw heads with roofing cement or caulk to prevent water damage
- Apply waterproofing (to restrict water entry) or reflective coatings (to reduce solar heat absorption) to roofs or other surfaces
- Follow applicable building codes

■ *Many roofers now install photovoltaic systems on roofs, such as the solar water panel heating component above.*

Green construction, or green building, is a relatively new concept that stresses energy and water efficiency, indoor environmental quality, the use of eco-friendly or fewer construction materials (when possible), and the structure's overall effects on its site or the larger community. Green roofers perform job duties such as:

- Installing **solar energy** roofing systems that have energy-collecting **photovoltaic** panels built into roofing membranes, tiles, or shingles

- Attaching solar panels to existing roofs

- Installing modular plant- and soil-holding systems over existing roof membranes to create green roofs; these systems include protective membranes, drainage and aeration components, water retention and filtering layers, soil substrates, irrigation materials, and plants

- Encouraging customers to install daylighting, which increases the admission of sunlight into a building to reduce electric lighting and save energy

- Suggesting the use of metal roofing over asphalt or tile roofing because it lasts longer and provides better protection than conventional roofing

Metal roofing systems were used in more than 11 percent of residential roofing projects in 2015, according to the Metal Roofing Alliance. This was an increase of 7 percent from 1998.

Green roofers seek to be eco-friendly by using energy-efficient roof membranes and low– or zero–volatile organic compound adhesives. They seek to recycle asphalt roofing shingles—along with other construction debris—instead of dumping them into landfills (places where garbage is dumped). Recycled shingles are used in asphalt pavement for roads and other purposes.

A career as a green roofer is a good option if you care about protecting the environment, are interested in learning about and using new technologies, enjoy solving unique design and installation problems, and like helping customers reduce energy waste and use alternative energy resources.

Work Environments

Roofers work outdoors in the blazing heat of summer or the chilly or even freezing days of spring, fall, and winter. In the winter in some northern climates, it is harder

■ *Roofers continue to work in the winter, although the job is much more challenging.*

to build new roofs, but far from impossible. A responsible roofer does not work in the rain or strong winds because the work environment is even more dangerous, the exposed roof deck (new construction) will absorb water and swell, and new shingles cannot be attached to wet wood (if this is done, mold and wood rot can develop). Smart roofers keep big tarps on hand in case they are surprised by an unexpected rain shower.

Work schedules vary for roofers, but most work forty hours a week, Monday through Friday. Some roofers work on weekends if they have many jobs to complete or they are trying to finish work before it rains or snows.

Roof construction sites can be loud, physically demanding, dirty, and dangerous. Some roofers wear earplugs to protect their hearing, and many wear protective gloves, hard hats, and safety goggles. Responsible roofers use fall protection systems, ladder tie-offs, high-traction roof boots, and other safety devices. Travel to various job sites is required, so you'll need a driver's license and a trustworthy vehicle.

■ *Learn about the work environment for roofers, the rewards of working in the field, and opportunities for advancement into roofing design and engineering:*

■ *Roofers with at least five years on the job and a strong track record can become foremen, who manage teams of roofers.*

Becoming a Boss

Roofers who have at least five years of experience can advance to the position of foreman. In this career, you'll manage a team of roofers and trainees as they repair or install roofs. Major job responsibilities for foremen include:

- Creating a work order and worker assignments to detail the work that needs to be done and who will be doing each task

- Before each work day, inspecting the job site to identify any safety issues that need to be addressed, and completing a daily hazard analysis form and submitting to site managers or the owner of the company

- Making sure that work crews meet project deadlines

- Lending a hand occasionally to help experienced roofers and trainees meet deadlines or cover worker absences

- Meeting with job superintendents during the project to make sure that the work is being completed on-budget, on-time, and meets other project guidelines

- Checking finished work to ensure that it meets applicable building codes and project specifications

- Preparing reports that summarize the work that was completed
- Ordering equipment and supplies, and maintaining company vehicles, as needed
- Evaluating the work of apprentices to ensure that their skills and knowledge of roofing materials and construction techniques are improving

If you enjoy managing others, can effectively deal with stress and deadlines, and are willing to travel to multiple construction sites to supervise work teams, you will be successful as a foreman. An experienced foreman can advance to the position of project superintendent or owner of a roofing construction firm. Others decide to become instructors in apprenticeship or technical programs, or pursue additional education to become roofing engineers.

Starting Your Own Contracting Business

Do you like making your own decisions and managing others? Are you good at math, business, and accounting? If so, you might have a future as a roofing business owner (also known as a contractor). Once you launch your business, you'll probably specialize in commercial or residential roofing, although some companies install and repair both types of roofing.

Being a business owner can be rewarding—and even fun—as you gradually get more clients, hire more roofers for your team, and build your company. You'll get to set your own hours, and you'll also have a chance to make more money than a roofer who works as an employee of a company.

But the sky is not always blue for roofing business owners. Storm clouds (difficult customers, clients who don't pay their bills, the pressure of managing office staff, the challenge of generating enough business to pay the bills and make payroll) often threaten, but if you plan well and work hard, you should be able to handle any problem that arises.

■ *One related career path for an experienced roofer is that of home inspector, who inspects roofs and other components of existing or newly constructed buildings.*

Related Career Paths

Roofers who complete additional education and training are qualified to work in many related fields. Additionally, their skills allow them to move on to some related jobs without pursuing more education. Here are a few popular options:

Construction inspectors examine buildings and other structures to ensure that they have been built correctly. *Building inspectors* examine homes, condominiums, town-homes, and other new or previously owned buildings. They are also known as *home inspectors*. Some inspectors specialize in examining the condition of existing or newly constructed roofs.

Solar photovoltaic installers build, install, and maintain solar panel systems. Some connect the solar arrays to the electric grid. They are employed by photovoltaic panel manufacturers; plumbing, heating, and air-conditioning contractors; electrical contractors and other wiring installation contractors; and power and communication line and related structures construction firms.

Framing carpenters measure, cut, and assemble wood and other materials to create the basic framework for floor, wall, and roof framing, window installation, and exterior door installation. They are also known as rough carpenters.

Signs That a Roof Needs Repair

- Leaks and water damage
- Buckling, curling, or blistering shingles
- Missing shingles or tiles
- Cracked tiles
- Loose material or wear around chimneys, pipes, and other components that enter the roof
- Large amounts of shingle granules in gutters (granules are used to add weight to shingles and protect them from damage by ultraviolet light)

Sheet metal workers cut and install products that are made of thin metal sheets, such as ductwork for heating, cooling, and refrigeration systems; rain gutters; roof flashing; siding; outdoor signs; and medical equipment.

Workplace Safety

The career of roofer ranks amongst the top five most-dangerous jobs in the United States, according to the U.S. Department of Labor. The most common injuries include:

- Broken bones, concussions, spinal cord injuries, and other injuries caused by falls from roofs, ladders, or scaffolds
- Cuts from sharp tools while hammering, sharp objects on the roof or ground, or from injuries that occurred while performing other tasks
- Burns from hot asphalt or other substances
- Heatstroke, heat exhaustion, and dehydration from work in extremely hot temperatures
- Serious sunburn
- Frostbite and hypothermia from working in extremely cold conditions
- Back injuries and muscle stress/strains
- Eye injuries caused by foreign objects entering the eyes

- Tendonitis, carpel tunnel syndrome, and pinched nerves caused by repetitive motions
- Respiratory issues due to exposure to hazardous chemicals and fumes, and other toxic or **carcinogenic substances**
- Knee, leg, or other injuries caused by kneeling for long periods or slipping on wet or icy surfaces
- Hearing damage caused by loud noise from cutting/sawing materials, drilling, hammering, or using nail guns

Other injuries are caused by electrocution, collapsing roofs and ladders, and malfunctioning equipment.

■ *Learn more about the importance of wearing safety gear when working on a roof:*

How to Stay Safe on the Job

Roofers must follow strong safety practices to avoid injury and even death (approximately fifty roofers die a year in the United States, according to the U.S. Department of Labor, most by falls). To stay safe, roofers wear safety glasses, respirators, earplugs, heavy gloves, protective clothing to prevent injury from temperature extremes, hardhats, and high-traction roof boots. To protect roofers from falls, some companies require the use of guardrails, safety nets, or personal fall-arrest systems, warning lines (to mark off roof-edge danger zones), and safety monitors (to warn workers when they are in danger). Here are a few safety measures to follow if you work as a roofer:

- Keep yourself in good physical shape so your body can withstand the physical demands of this work.

- At the beginning of each work day, inspect your job site to identify potential hazards (broken equipment, slippery work areas, etc.) and fix them.

- Use a ladderlift, a human-, electrical-, or battery-powered device that transports heavy building materials up a ladder to a roof or other high area.

- Stay focused on the job to avoid falls, cuts, burns, bumps and bruises, and other injuries.

- Use a respirator, an artificial breathing device that will protect you from breathing in dust, asphalt fumes, or other toxic substances such as asbestos, lead, and silica.

- Make sure your tools and equipment are in good working order.

- Use ladder tie-offs, straps that secure ladders to a roof or structure.

- To avoid electrocution, be very careful when you work around overhead power lines.

- Address your concerns about project safety with your foreman or the job superintendent.

■ *Following safety procedures is extremely important because roofers spend most of their time working at heights. Above, a roofer wears a safety harness to protect him from a fall.*

Roofers and Noise Protection

The Center for Construction Research and Training conducted an industry-wide survey in 2016 and 2017 to gather information on workers' knowledge about the dangers of workplace noise. It found that while 70.5 percent of roofers said that they had received training on how to wear hearing protection, only 8 percent always or most always wore hearing protection gear on the job. Fifty percent said they wore ear protection never or almost never, 31 percent some of the time, and 11 percent most of the time. Respondents said that they did not wear ear protection because they believed it kept them from communicating effectively at job sites, because it was not provided, or because no one else was wearing ear protection.

Text-Dependent Questions

1. What do commercial roofers do?

2. What are some signs that a roof needs to be repaired?

3. What kinds of safety gear do roofers use to protect themselves on the job?

Research Project

Develop your building skills by constructing a clubhouse or treehouse in your backyard. Read *Keep Out!: Build Your Own Backyard Clubhouse: A Step-by-Step Guide*, by Lee Mothes, and check out YouTube.com for step-by-step directions. Be sure to work with your parents on this project.

CHAPTER 2
Tools of the Trade

Demolition, Cleaning, Repair, and Construction Tools

airless sprayer: A mechanical device that is used to apply liquid coating to a roof surface.

caulk gun: A manual tool that holds a tube or cartridge that is filled with caulk (a waterproof filler and sealant, usually silicone or latex); the gun is used to fill cracks and gaps during construction projects, as well as bond materials such as metal, glass, wood, and ceramics.

chalk line: A marking tool that is used to snap horizontal and vertical chalk lines on the roof deck or to measure exact shingle positioning.

crowbar: A metal bar with a single curved end and flattened points that is used to pry up shingles, nails, and other building materials.

drill: A hand or power tool that is fitted with a cutting tool attachment or driving tool attachment; it is used to cut into material ranging from wood and stone, to metal and plastic.

hammer: A hand tool with a metal or wooden head that is mounted to the handle at right angles; it is used to drive or remove nails or break-up old construction materials.

hammer tacker: A tool that drives wire staples into roofing felt, insulation, or other materials to connect them to other building materials.

nail gun: A power tool that is used to quickly drive nails into wood or other construction materials.

roller: A hand-held device that is used to apply adhesives.

shingle hog: An air compressor-powered machine (that looks somewhat like a small snow blower) that is used to remove a large number of shingles at one time.

snips: A hand-held tool that is used to cut asphalt or fiberglass shingles, or other materials.

spud bar: A long-handled, flat-bladed device that is used to chip and loosen embedded aggregate and for prying up sections of a built-up roof.

staple gun: A tool that drives wire staples into roofing felt or other building materials.

stiff-bristle hand broom: A tool that is used to sweep gravel and loose debris from a roof surface.

straight-blade knife: A hand tool that is used to cut shingles and other materials.

tear-off bar: A tool with a long handle and a steel blade that is used to remove shingles and nails.

turbo shear: A metal-cutting device that makes straight, curved, or square cuts in most metal sheets. It is powered via an attachment to a drill.

Safety and Access Gear and Equipment

dust mask: A protective covering worn over the mouth and nose to reduce the inhalation of dust and other airborne pollutants.

fall protection systems: A collection of equipment and gear that helps roofers and other construction workers to stay safe on the job. They usually include a reusable roof anchor, safety harness, rope lifeline, and shock-absorbing lanyard (a cord or strap worn around the body).

high-traction roof boots: Footwear that is specially designed to allow roofers and other workers to walk on roofs without slipping.

ladder: A device that is made out of metal, wood, or other materials that is used to climb up or down.

ladderlift: A human-, electrical-, or battery-powered device that transports heavy building materials up a ladder to a roof or other high area.

ladder tie-offs: Straps that secure ladders to a roof or structure. They keep the ladder from being blown down by strong winds and prevent it from slipping away from the building as a person climbs it.

respirator: An artificial breathing device that protects the wearer from breathing dust, smoke, or other toxic substances.

safety glasses: Protective gear that shields the eyes of trades workers from injury by protruding nails, sharp edges, and wires, as well as from sparks given off by short circuits on electrical panels.

Computer Technology

building information modeling software: A computer application that uses a 3D model-based process that helps construction, architecture, and engineering professionals to more efficiently plan, design, build, and manage buildings and infrastructure.

moisture meter: A handheld device that can either find elevated moisture levels hidden behind building materials, or actually measure the elevated moisture levels by touching the material with two pins on the device. Some meters can perform both functions.

office and customer management software: A computer application that helps users track finances and manage billing, draft correspondence, and perform other tasks.

thermal imaging scanner: A device used by roofers, HVACR technicians, electricians, home inspectors, and others to find moisture intrusion, detect energy loss/missing insulation, and perform other functions.

CHAPTER 3

Terms of the Trade

adhesive: A substance such as glue or contact cement that can be used to bond material together by surface attachment.

asphalt shingle: A type of roofing shingle that is made from a mixture of dark bituminous pitch and gravel or sand. Asphalt shingles are one of the most commonly-used types of shingles, and they are often used on sloped roofs and residential projects.

batten: A strip of wood, plastic, metal, or fiberglass that provides an attachment point for tiles, and that is used to hold down felt.

blistering: An unwanted bubbling of roofing materials (such as shingles) that is caused by either moisture under the material or moisture trapped inside the material.

blow-offs: The loss of shingles or tiles from a roof when they are blown off by high winds.

building codes: A series of rules established by local, state, regional, and national governments that ensure safe construction.

caulk: Waterproof filler and sealant that is used to fill spaces around the base of the chimney, along the walls and around plumbing vents, and other areas. Deteriorating caulking can allow the intrusion of water and cause damage to ceilings, walls, and other building components.

ceiling joist: A construction component that connects the outside walls, supports the ceiling for the room below, and secures the bottom ends of the rafters. If one views the roof structure as an equilateral triangle, the rafters would make up the top left and right segments of the triangle, and the ceiling joist the bottom segment.

corrosion: A chemical reaction that causes deterioration of metal (such as a steel roof), stone, or other materials.

cupping: An unwanted curling that occurs on shingles when they are improperly installed over an existing roof. The issue may also be caused by a manufacturing defect.

eaves: The areas of the roof where it meets or overhangs the walls of a building.

fasteners: Nails or staples that are used to affix felt, shingles, or other materials on a roof.

fiberglass shingle: A type of asphalt shingle that lasts fifteen to thirty years.

flashing: Sheet metal that is used to prevent the entry of water at wall and roof junctions and around chimneys. It is installed underneath the siding and shingles.

gutter: A long trough and a drainage pipe that removes water from roofs.

ice damming: The buildup of ice and water at the eaves (where the roof meets or overhangs the walls of a building) of a sloped roof. It is caused by inadequate attic insulation or ventiation and other factors.

joists: A series of parallel, horizontal components of wood, engineered wood, or steel that supports a ceiling or floor. Joists are supported by beams, wall framing, and foundations.

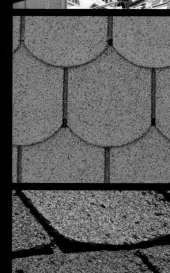

masonry: Construction using durable materials such as tile, brick, cement, stone (marble, granite, limestone, etc.), or similar materials.

nail-pop: An unwanted issue that occurs when a nail is not fully driven; it sits above the roof deck.

overdriven: A term that is used when nails, staples, or other fasteners are driven through roofing material with too much force, causing damage to the material.

pitch: In construction, the angle of rise in degrees from a horizontal starting point. The degree of pitch is an important consideration in roof construction because it affects the type of construction materials that are used, water drainage considerations, and the amount of room in the upper story or attic of a building.

proud: Slang for when one building component protrudes above another.

rafter: A sloping framing component that runs downward from the peak of the roof to the ceiling joist. If one views the roof structure as an equilateral triangle, the rafters would make up the top left and right segments of the triangle, and the ceiling joist the bottom segment.

roofing felt: A layer of protection installed between the roof deck and the roofing shingles. The felt repels water, provides backup protection in the event of damage to or loss of shingles, and serves other functions. Also known as **roofing felt underlayment, roofing tar paper,** and **roll roofing.**

roofing membrane: A layer or layers of waterproofing products (often made from synthetic rubber, thermoplastic, or modified bitumen) that cover and move water from the roof.

roofing nail: A nail that has a wide flat head and short shank. Roofing nails are used to install shingles, fasten roofing felt, attach roof flashing, and for other uses. Also known as **clout nails.**

roof deck: The base of the roof (which is usually constructed with plywood, wood boards, or planks) over which roofing materials are applied.

roof tile: An alternate material that is used to cover a roof and keep out moisture. Roof tiles are made from terracotta, slate, concrete, plastic, and other materials.

scaffold: A temporary raised structure that roofers and other trades workers use to work at heights that would otherwise be hard to reach.

sheathing: Wood that is placed on top of the rafters to add rigidity to the roof frame and provide a nailing surface for fasteners. It is often required by building code.

shingle: A small, thin covering that protects homes from water infiltration and other issues. A series of shingles make up a roof. Shingles are made from asphalt, wood, or other substances.

shingle buckling: The unwanted bending of a shingle because of movement in the roof sheathing due to changes in moisture levels, wetting of the felt paper (which will expand if it gets wet), and other factors.

solar module: An energy-efficient component that is placed on a roof to collect the sun's energy to heat or cool a building.

tear-off: The removal of existing roofing materials down to the roof deck.

truss: A structural framework of wood that serves to bridge the space above a room and support the roof.

underdriven: A term that is used when nails, staples, or other fasteners are not fully driven flush to a shingle's surface.

■ *Shop classes provide an excellent introduction to the construction industry.*

Words to Understand

apprenticeship: A formal training program that combines classroom instruction and supervised practical experience. Apprentices are paid a salary that increases as they obtain experience.

at-will employee: A non-union worker who can be fired at any time for almost any reason.

community college: A private or public two-year college that awards certificates and associate degrees. A small number of community colleges award bachelor's degrees.

technical school: A public or private college that offers two- or four-year programs in practical subjects, such as the trades, information technology, applied sciences, agriculture, and engineering.

CHAPTER 4

Preparing for the Field and Making a Living

Educational Paths

There are many ways to prepare to become a roofer. Most aspiring roofers learn their skills through on-the-job training, while others learn through an apprenticeship or by attending a technical school or community college. Some people choose to get a head start on their training by taking high school classes and participating in pre-apprenticeship programs.

High School Classes

Shop classes will provide an excellent introduction to the construction industry. You'll learn how to use hand and power tools to cut, shape, and otherwise work with metal, wood, stone, and other building materials. You'll also develop your troubleshooting and problem-solving skills as you build and repair things. Other topics that you'll learn about include blueprint reading and estimating, energy efficiency and green construction techniques, safety practices, and national and local building codes.

■ *The Pythagorean Theorem.*

Math classes are important, too, because roofers use math every day on the job. For example, they use basic math to assess distances between structural components and determine the amount of shingles or tiles that are needed. They also use the Pythagorean Theorem to determine the length of rafters. Roofers who own

The Pythagorean Theorem

 The Pythagorean Theorem states that the sum of the squares of the lengths of the legs of a right triangle ("a" and "b" in the triangle shown on page 33) is equal to the square of the length of the hypotenuse ("c"). It is often written as a2 + b2 = c2.

Source: MathForum.org

their own contracting businesses use mathematics to determine estimates, prepare billing, create payroll, and perform many other tasks. Other useful classes for future business owners include computer science, business, accounting, current events, English, and writing.

Physical education classes will help you to develop your strength, agility, and stamina—traits you'll need on the job as a roofer.

You should also consider learning a foreign language, such as Spanish (if you live in the United States), because many roofing professionals do not speak English fluently or at all. *Contractor Supply* estimates that nearly 50 percent of roofers in the United States are Latino. While some may be fluent in English, others may not be.

On-the-Job Training

The majority of roofers trained for the field by working as roofing laborers, learning on the job from experienced roofers. This type of training lasts from one to three years. In the beginning, you'll probably just fetch tools and supplies; set up ladders, hoists, and scaffolds; prepare roofs for shingling or tiling; and clean up roofing debris. Eventually, you'll be asked to measure, cut, and fit roofing materials, and then be taught how to lay shingles and tiles. During this time, it's also a good idea to take classes on roofing and general construction practices that are offered by professional associations and technical and community colleges. This will help you to both expand your knowledge and impress your bosses with your dedication to improve your skills.

Learning on the job is a good approach if you want to get to work right away and receive a salary, you do not need a structured educational setting to learn, and you are able to pick up your skills and knowledge on the job. Drawbacks to this approach

■ *On-the-job training allows aspiring roofers to get right to work and build their skills.*

include training that might not be as detailed as what you would obtain in an apprenticeship or degree program, and that you might have to do entry-level tasks for a long time before you are trusted with shingling or tiling a roof.

Pre-Apprenticeships

If you decide to train to become a roofer by participating in an apprenticeship program, it's a good idea to participate in a pre-apprenticeship program first. Such programs allow you to determine if a career in roofing (and the overall construction industry) is how you want to spend the rest of your work life. Pre-apprenticeship programs are offered by professional associations, community colleges, and unions. For example, the Canadian Roofing Contractors' Association and Canadian Council of Sheet Metal Workers & Roofers offer a pre-apprenticeship training program for roofers. In the first part of the program, which lasts one day, trainees learn basic safety and construction practices before they begin work at a construction site. The final component of the training involves up to thirty additional hours of instruction at the job site. Trainees learn more about safety and become familiar with the tools and equipment used in roofing construction and repair. They work with a mentor journey person or experienced roofer on the construction of one type of roofing system

■ *Many roofers prepare for the field via apprenticeships.*

(modified bitumen membrane, single-ply thermoplastic, single-ply thermoset, steep, etc.). When the trainee completes the educational and training requirements, he or she receives a pre-apprenticeship certificate that is recognized by companies across Canada. In some provinces, this experience can be transferred to an advanced standing in an apprenticeship program.

In the United States, Associated Builders and Contractors offers a pre-apprenticeship program that prepares students to enter a registered apprenticeship program. Some of the modules completed by participants include:

- Introduction to Construction Math
- Introduction to Hand Tools
- Introduction to Power Tools
- Introduction to Construction Drawings
- Introduction to Material Handling
- Pipes and Fittings

The National Association of Home Builders offers pre-apprenticeship certificate training through the Home Builders Institute. The program is geared toward high school and college students, transitioning military members, veterans, justice-involved youth and adults, and unemployed and displaced workers. Programs are available in carpentry, building construction technology, weatherization, masonry, electrical, landscaping, plumbing, and painting.

■ *Learn more about the many benefits of participating in a roofing apprenticeship:*

■ *Fellow apprentices can be important members of your professional network.*

Apprenticeships

The United Union of Roofers, Waterproofers and Allied Workers offers an apprenticeship training program for roofers. The program lasts three-and-a-half years and provides on-the-job training during the day and classes in the evening. Apprentices learn about site preparation, rigging and hoisting, roofing materials, safety practices, roof systems, roof repair and maintenance, calculations and architectural drawings, green roofing, how to protect roofing from ultraviolet rays and other environmental hazards, and other topics. In the United States, apprentices typically complete 2,000 hours of on-the-job training and 144 hours of related classroom instruction each year in the program. Visit http://www.doleta.gov/OA/sainformation.cfm for information on apprenticeship training programs in the United States.

Entry requirements vary by program, but typical requirements include:

- Minimum age of eighteen
- High school education
- One year of high school algebra

- Qualifying score on an aptitude test
- No use of illegal drugs

In Canada, the length of apprenticeship training programs varies, but generally involves four twelve-month periods, including at least 5,860 hours of on-the-job training, three six-week blocks of technical training, and a final certificate exam. If you live outside the U.S. or Canada, contact your nation's department of labor to learn more about training programs.

■ *Learn how a roofing apprentice developed social skills during his apprenticeship:*

As apprentices gain experience, they receive more responsibility and higher pay. Those who complete an apprenticeship program are known as journeymen roofers. In some U.S. states and other countries, roofers must be licensed or registered. Roofers who are licensed have passed exams and met other requirements to show that they are skilled at their jobs. Registration is much different. It just requires that there is a written record of who is performing the roofing work. Just because someone is registered does not mean that they are highly skilled.

Participating in an apprenticeship is a good approach because it provides a clear path to employment. Unlike traditional college programs, you'll get paid while you learn (although many programs require apprentices to purchase their own tools), and your earnings increase as you gain experience. An apprenticeship is a good option for those who like a structured learning environment that combines both classroom and hands-on training.

Technical and Community College

Some aspiring roofers prepare for the field by combining on-the-job training in roofing with classes in roofing, carpentry, and other construction trades from a technical college or community college. Others attend school, but do not work yet in the industry. Some roofers also choose to earn certificates, technical diplomas, and/ or associate degrees in construction technology, carpentry, and other trades-related fields. Some programs are affiliated with unions (organizations of trades workers that seek to gain better wages, benefits, and working conditions for their members) or contractor organizations.

Going the college route is a good choice if you want to enter the workforce more quickly than if you participated in an apprenticeship. The drawbacks: you must pay tuition and you do not get paid like apprentices do. (Note: If you participate in a college program that combines classes and an apprenticeship program, you will receive pay.)

Getting a Job

Once you complete your educational program, you'll either be offered a job through your apprenticeship or on-the-job training program, or you'll have to look for a job. Here are some popular job-search methods:

Use Your Network. Eighty-five percent of all jobs are filled via networking, according to workplace studies. Networking just involves telling people that you are looking for a job, asking for information about roofing companies and the industry as a whole, and helping others find jobs if you can do so. You have two types of networks: personal and professional. Your personal network consists of friends and family. Your professional network consists of the following types of people:

- Fellow apprentices and classmates
- Instructors
- Job superintendents
- People you meet at roofing industry events
- People you meet online, including at social networking sites such as LinkedIn.

Check Out Job Boards. Job listings can be found on internet job boards that are hosted by professional associations, government agencies, and businesses. At many

Roofing Industry Certifications

 Industry associations offer voluntary certifications for roofers. They provide a good way for roofers to stand out from the crowd and show potential customers that they have special skills and have met high standards of ability. Those who are certified typically earn higher salaries and have better job prospects than those who are not certified. The National Roofing Contractors Association, which has members in the United States and more than fifty other countries, offers the following credentials:

- ProForeman Certificate
- Certified Roofing Torch Applicator
- Future Executives Institute
- Executive Management Institute Certificate
- Certified Solar Roofing Professional

of these sites, you can search by geographic region, salary, job type, employer name, and other criteria. While you're not ready to look for a job, it never hurts to read some job listings to see what types of duties, skills, and educational backgrounds are in demand. Here are a few popular job boards:

- http://www.nrca.net/Careers
- http://www.unionroofers.com/Jobs/Help-Wanted.aspx
- https://www.linkedin.com
- https://www.usajobs.gov (U.S. government job board)
- https://www.jobbank.gc.ca (Canadian government job board)
- https://www.gov.uk/jobsearch (United Kingdom government job board).

Join and Use the Resources of Unions and Professional Associations. A union is an organization of workers that seeks to gain better wages, benefits, and working conditions for its members. They are also called *labor unions* or *trade unions*. It's estimated that about 15 percent of roofers in the United States are members of unions. The main union for roofers in the United States is the United Union of

Roofers, Waterproofers & Allied Workers. Some roofers in the U.S. and Canada are members of the International Association of Sheet Metal, Air, Rail and Transportation Workers. Other countries also have unions for roofing professionals. Benefits of union membership include:

- Higher earnings, better benefits, and more job security than those who are not members of unions
- Access to union-sponsored continuing education and leadership development programs, support and representation if they have problems at work (discrimination, unfair labor practices, etc.)
- Access to many networking and job-search contacts
- Cannot be fired without "just cause," unlike **at-will employees**. This means that there must be a good reason (breaking rules, etc.) that they are fired.

A professional association is a private organization of people in a specific industry (information technology, construction, etc.) or career (nurses, roofers, etc.). The association exists to provide membership, protect the rights of workers or larger industry, education programs, networking opportunities, and other resources. Most countries

■ *A roofing engineer draws up plans for a roof.*

Roofer Career Path

Roofing Engineer: Studies damaged roofs on industrial, commercial, and residential buildings to establish cause and extent of failure or damage; suggest strategies to repair the damage. A minimum of a bachelor's degree is required to enter this career, but a master's degree is preferred.

Business Owner: Operates a contracting firm that provides services to homeowners and businesses. Business owners may have a degree in business management.

Foreman: A journeyman roofer who manages a group of other journeymen and apprentices on a project.

Journeyman Roofer: Has completed an apprenticeship or other training. If licensed, can work without direct supervision.

Apprentice Roofer: Requirements vary by country. In the United States, apprentice roofers complete 2,000 hours of on-the-job training and 144 hours of related classroom instruction during each year of a three-and-a-half-year course of study.

have at least one professional association for roofers. For example, major roofing and construction organizations in the United States include the National Roofing Contractors Association, Associated General Contractors of America, Asphalt Roofing Manufacturers Association, Home Builders Institute, and National Association of Home Builders. Other countries such as Canada (Canadian Roofing Contractors' Association), Australia (Roofing Tile Association of Australia and the Metal Roofing and Cladding Association of Australia), and United Kingdom (National Federation of Roofing Contractors Limited) have their own trade associations.

How Much Can I Earn?

A career in roofing is definitely not one of the highest-paying jobs in the construction industry. In fact, roofers earn average pay (about $42,100 in the United States), which typically falls at the lower end of the pay scale for trades workers. The average pay for all construction workers in the U.S. is $48,900. Ten percent of all roofers (typically those without much experience) earn $25,040 a year. Roofers who are certified can increase their earnings.

Roofers who work for certain types of employers earn higher average salaries than those in other sectors. The U.S. Department of Labor reports the following average annual earnings for roofers by employer:

- Local government agencies: $61,360
- Nonresidential building construction firms: $49,650
- Residential building construction firms: $49,030
- Foundation, structure, and building exterior contractors: $41,760
- Building finishing contractors: $40,150.

Average Salaries for Trades Workers in the United States

Salaries for roofers are not as high as those in many other trades careers. Here's how their pay ranks compared to other trades workers.

- Elevator Installers and Repairers: $76,860
- Electricians: $56,650
- Plumbers, Pipefitters, and Steamfitters: $56,030
- Brickmasons and Blockmasons: $53,440
- Sheet Metal Workers: $51,080
- Carpenters: $48,340
- Heating and Cooling Technicians: $48,320
- Tile and Marble Setters: $44,770
- Plasterers and Stucco Masons: $44,070
- Roofers: $42,080
- Painters and Paperhangers: $41,430

■ *The United Union of Roofers, Waterproofers & Allied Workers reports that wages for roofing apprentices can be as high as $35 per hour, but typically average around $20 per hour.*

Salaries for Helpers and Apprentices

Some roofers prepare for the field by working as helpers at job sites. Roofing helpers earn average salaries of $27,670, according to the USDL. Earnings range from less than $20,330 to $39,110 or more.

The United Union of Roofers, Waterproofers & Allied Workers reports that wages for roofing apprentices vary based on the geographic location of the local union. It estimates that they can be as high as $35 per hour, but typically average around $20 per hour.

Salaries for Roofers by U.S. State

Earnings for roofers vary widely by state based on demand and other factors. Here are the five states where employers pay the highest average salary and the states in which employers pay the lowest salaries.

Highest Average Salaries:

1. New York: $62,880

2. New Jersey: $59,260

3. Minnesota: $57,710

4. Connecticut: $54,380

5. Illinois: $54,130

Lowest Average Salaries:

1. South Dakota: $30,570

2. Mississippi: $31,090

3. New Mexico: $31,240

4. Alabama: $31,810

5. Florida: $32,510

Source: U.S. Department of Labor

Top Earners

The top 10 percent of roofers earn $64,630 or more, according to the USDL. These high-paid workers typically have a lot of experience, are very skilled at their work, have supervisory or managerial duties, or live in large cities and other areas with high demand for roofers and a shortage of workers.

Roofing foremen earn median salaries of $48,664, according to PayScale.com. Salaries range from $29,233 to $70,957 or more.

Roofing contractors with successful businesses can earn $90,000 to $200,000 or more, depending on the size of their companies.

Union members often receive medical insurance, a pension, and other benefits from their union. Roofers who work for large contractors may receive these and other benefits. Self-employed workers must provide their own fringe benefits.

Text-Dependent Questions

1. What high school classes should you take to prepare for training to become a roofer?

2. What is the most popular training method for aspiring roofers, and how long does this training last?

3. What is the average salary for a roofer in the United States?

Research Project

Talk to roofers who trained for the field in different ways (apprenticeship, on-the-job training, community or technical college) to learn what they liked and disliked about their training. Write a report that summarizes the pros and cons of each training method.

ON THE JOB

Interview with a Professional

Rob LaBelle is the owner and founder of LaBelle Roofing, Inc. (https://www.labelleroofing.com) in Wayland, Massachusetts. He started his company in 2007.

Q. What made you to get into this field?

A. I started off as a laborer in the building trades, doing general remodeling of residential homes. I obtained my construction supervisors license, and then I got a sales position (in-home sales) selling residential roofing installations for a national company. I always have had an entrepreneurial spirit and after a short stint selling roofing (1.5 years) I decided to strike out on my own. I felt I had the skills to make it in the very competitive roofing market. I tend to be an independent-minded person and honestly didn't enjoy working for others. I had some negative experiences at my job. I was thirty-eight years old when I began. I guess the reason I chose roofing was because that is what I was most familiar with. My intent was to run a business, not "own a job." The fact of the matter is that roofing is tough work, and I never planned on swinging a hammer. I had aches and pains and really didn't even like heights, truth be told.

Q. Can you tell me about a day in your life on the job?

A. As a business owner, my daily activities consist of constantly working on the business, not in it. I have made it my mission to read all I can on running a small business. One of my favorite concepts that many books stress is exactly this: working on the business, not in it. Setting up systems and then testing and refining them is mostly what I do. I am always looking for ideas and technology that can help our company to become more effective and efficient at what we do.

Q. What is the most rewarding part of your job?

A. I think the most rewarding part of my job is the creativity that allows me to visualize and achieve small goals, little by little. I enjoy looking back year after year at the progress we have made. I enjoy the freedom that being a business owner allows me. I am open to and take input from employees on how to get better at what we do. Ultimately though, I get to have the final say and control my own destiny. Earning more money is another very rewarding aspect of being in business. I started LaBelle Roofing when I was in considerable debt. In the last eleven years, I have been able to turn that around. I do not believe that I could have gotten where I have financially without having went into business for myself.

Q. What kind of personal traits do you think are important for roofing professionals?

A. I think the most important personal trait that leads to success in business is loving the process. I am not a roofer. I am a business owner. I love running and growing my business—it's fun. I think that honesty, integrity, and a strong work ethic—along with persistence—are all you really need. Persistence is key. Early on, I wanted to give up a few times. It was not easy to hang in there. In the beginning, I started with nothing. I worked seven days a week for the first three years and, many days, I worked for twelve to fifteen hours or more to get the business off the ground. I always kept in mind the adage that "it takes more fuel to get a jet airplane off the ground than it does to fly across the country." You need to be able to hang in there, and it is worth the effort.

Q. What advice would you give to someone who is considering a career as a roofing contractor?

A. If you want to be a contractor of any kind, a business owner, then learn all you can about the various aspects of running a business. *The E-Myth Revisited: Why Most Small Businesses Don't Work and What to Do About It* is a good book to check out, but there are hundreds of books that will inspire you and help you to get prepared for everything you need to know. There is no substitute for experience, and this only comes with time. The important thing is to not give-up! Spend as much time as you can visualizing how you want the business to be, to function. Find someone who is doing what you want to do, and who is successful doing it. Then do what they do, and you will get the same result. Always do the right thing, be ethical, and you will win. Get a bookkeeper from day one and know your numbers! Understanding your costs and profit margins, and having the data you need to adjust accordingly is huge. Understand the difference between an asset and a liability; check out Robert Kiyosaki (http://www.richdad.com), he is one of the best. By all means, start a business. It's one of the best ways to make a lot of money.

■ *Roofers must have excellent balance because they not only have to work at heights, but often use a variety of tools while doing so.*

Words to Understand

computer-aided design: The use of computer software to design and develop products and floor and building plans.

ethnic group: A collection of people who have a shared connection based on their homeland, cultural heritage, history, ancestry, language, or other factors.

invoicing: The process of sending a customer a bill for work that has been completed.

nonprofit organization: A group (unlike a corporation or other for-profit business) that uses any profits it generates to advance its stated goals (protecting the environment, helping the homeless, etc.).

CHAPTER 5

Key Skills and Methods of Exploration

What All Roofers Need

- When you think of key traits for roofers, most people would say "strong," "good balance," and "not afraid of heights." While these traits are very important, roofers need many other skills— from the ability to work as a member of a team to excellent troubleshooting skills. Here are some key personal skills and physical traits for roofers:

- **Physical stamina.** As a roofer, you will work outside all day in the elements. This means working on roofs on hot, humid summer days, and on brisk fall days, and sometimes even in freezing temperatures. Throughout the day, you'll be climbing up and

■ *Roofers must be able to work well on their own.*

down ladders, bending, stooping, reaching, and performing repetitive movements. Being in good physical shape will make these tasks much easier.

- **Physical strength.** You will need to be able to lift and carry heavy materials. Some roofers must carry heavy sheets of plywood or bundles of shingles that weigh sixty pounds (27.2155 kilograms) or more. Ladderlifts and other lifting devices have been developed to help roofers carry tools and building materials up to a roof and to bring roofing debris down more easily, but not every roofing company uses this equipment.

- **Balance.** You need excellent balance to avoid falling off ladders and steep or slippery roofs.

- **Unafraid of heights.** This is not the career for you if you break into a cold sweat when you climb a ladder, or you stand on the observation deck of a tall building. You must not be afraid of heights because much of your work will be done twenty feet (6.096 meters) or more off the ground.

- **Detail-oriented.** Throughout the entire building process, roofers need to be attentive to detail. If you fail to install shingles or tiles correctly, for example, water could leak through the roof into the home and cause damage. If you own a roofing business, you'll need to keep detailed records regarding service calls, equipment and supplies used, and client **invoicing** and billing.

- **Time management.** You'll need to work quickly and keep track of time to get your assignment done quickly so that your team can move forward in the next step of the building process.

■ *The fear of heights is known as acrophobia.*

The fear of heights is known as acrophobia. Approximately 24 percent of Americans are afraid of heights, according to the Chapman University Survey of American Fears.

- **Troubleshooting ability.** When repairing a roof, you'll need to use your analytical abilities to identify problems. These range from the obvious (damaged or missing shingles or tiles) to those (rotted wood and finding the exact spot of a water leak) that require a little detective work. Additionally, challenges arise during any construction project, so you'll need to be good at identifying issues and developing creative solutions to solve them.

- **Teamwork and interpersonal skills.** Roofing teams usually include people of different ages, backgrounds, **ethnic groups**, and experience levels. Some may not even speak the main language or languages of your country. For this reason, you will need to work hard to connect with your teammates and understand and respect your differences, as well as try to find common ground, to get the job done.

- **Ability to work independently.** Most roofers work as a member of a team—whether that team consists of three or four roofers for a small, residential project, to a team of dozens for a large commercial project. But there will be many times when you are assigned a specific job duty and trusted to get the job done. For that reason, you'll need to be a good time manager, work effectively without supervision, and be comfortable solving problems on your own.

- **Communication and customer service skills.** Roofing is dangerous work, so you'll need strong communication skills to convey important information to your coworkers and explain any issues that arise to the foreman or business owner. If you own or manage a roofing business, you'll frequently meet with customers to explain the problems that you've identified with an existing roof and detail the steps that will be taken to build a new roof, explain the types of roofing materials, provide more information on a quote, and answer any customer questions. You'll also need patience to deal with customers who question the quality of your work (or its cost). Other key traits include punctuality, a friendly personality, and good listening skills.

■ *Computer science classes will come in handy, especially if you own your own roofing business.*

- **Technical and computer skills.** You'll need to be familiar with the latest testing equipment such as moisture meters, thermal imaging scanners, and other technology. Some roofers use **computer-aided design** software to design new roofs, and many business owners use software that helps them create estimates, manage budgets and billing, draft correspondence, and perform other tasks.

- **Business skills.** If you own a roofing business, you'll need to develop a wide range of skills, from preparing estimates for jobs and managing staff, to marketing your business on social media and through direct mail, and scheduling work appointments.

Exploring Roofing as a Student

There are many ways to learn about roofing, careers in the field, and the construction industry in general while you're still in school. Avoid heading up to a roof to look around (especially without supervision from an adult), but more down-to-earth options include classes, clubs, and competitions, do-it-yourself activities, and information interviews. Here are some popular methods of exploration:

Take Some Classes. Take shop class because roofers must be comfortable using power and hand tools and building and repairing things. In shop class you'll also learn about building codes and regulations, safety practices, and much more. Other useful classes include:

- **Mathematics:** Roofers use basic math every day to determine the slope of a roof, estimate how many shingles or tiles they'll need to cover a roof, and complete other calculations. If you own a business, you'll use your mathematical skills to maintain financial records, prepare estimates and payroll, and to accomplish other tasks.

- **Physics:** You will need to have a basic understanding of nature and the properties of matter and energy. Physics deal with such things as mechanics, heat, sound, electricity, light and other radiation, magnetism, and the structure of atoms.

- **English/writing:** You'll need to be able to effectively communicate both in writing and orally to coworkers and clients.

- **Computer science:** Roofers use various technologies to test for the presence of water or energy loss. Some use computer-aided design software to create the plans for new roofs. If you operate your own business, using estimation, project management, billing, and other types of software will make your job much easier.

- **Business, marketing, and accounting:** These classes will come in handy if you plan to start your own company.

■ *Get some hands-on experience by learning how to use a chalk line:*

■ *A student tries out a nail gun.*

Try Out Some Tools. It might be hard to get your hands on a thermal imaging scanner and other complex tools, but roofers use many basic tools such as a nail gun, roofing hammer, chalk line, or shingle remover that you might find in your parents' garage, at a hardware store, or at a local library (some have tool lending programs). Maybe you could even build a treehouse or fort in your backyard with the help of your parents, and experiment by using these and other tools to build its roof. The key is to become comfortable using these tools, while having fun in the process. Check out YouTube if you're not sure how to use certain tools.

Tour a Construction Site. One of the best ways to learn about a career in roofing is to observe roofers at work. For safety reasons, you won't be able to get up on a roof, but you can watch roofers at work from below. Or, if you live in a big city, perhaps you could view the construction of the roof of a smaller building from the indoor viewing deck of a taller one. Ask your shop teacher or school counselor to arrange a tour. Some industry organizations (such as Go Construct in the United Kingdom and Associated Construction Contractors of New Jersey in the United States) arrange tours to teach young people about construction specialties. Another strategy is to email or call local construction associations and trade unions to see if they organize tours. Since there is a shortage of many types of trades workers, many organizations will be happy to help you learn more about the industry.

When you arrive on your tour, try to ask these and other questions:

- What is being built? How long will it take to build?

- How many people are working on this project? How many of these workers are roofers?

- What type of roof is being built, and what types of building materials will be used in its construction?

- What have been the greatest design and construction challenges workers have faced in building the roof (as well as the entire building)? What unexpected problems arose, and how were they solved?

- Are there any green or sustainable design features incorporated into the roof (and in the project as a whole)?

■ *Touring a construction site is an excellent way to learn more about a career as a roofer and other opportunities in the trades.*

Join or Start a Construction Club at Your School. Is there a roofing club at your school? Probably not. But many schools offer construction clubs for those interested in building things and learning more about a career in the trades. By joining such a club, you'll learn more about different trades careers (such as roofer, mason, carpenter, and electrician), get a chance to try out tools and build things, possibly tour construction sites, and view presentations by construction professionals. If there's no construction club at your school, ask your shop teacher for help starting one. Or start your own with a group of like-minded friends.

Participate in a Competition. Competing in a contest is a good way to make new friends, build your skills, and test your abilities against students from around the country or world. Competitions are sponsored by schools, local park districts, trade associations, companies, or regional, national, or international membership organizations for young people. Here are two well-known organizations that host competitions that will allow you to develop and demonstrate your construction knowledge and skills:

- **SkillsUSA** (http://www.skillsusa.org) is a "national membership organization serving middle-school, high-school, and college/postsecondary students who are preparing for careers in trade, technical, and skilled service occupations." Its SkillsUSA Championships involve competitions in one hundred events. Students first compete locally, with winners advancing to state and national levels. A small number of winners can even advance to compete against young people from more than seventy-five other countries at WorldSkills International, which was recently held in Abu Dhabi, United Arab Emirates, and in Leipzig, Germany. SkillsUSA doesn't offer competitions for aspiring roofers, but it does offer contests in other fields that will help you to develop your construction and building skills. Some of these include Architectural Drafting, Carpentry, Engineering Technology/Design, Masonry, Principles of Engineering/Technology, Related Technical Math, Sheet Metal, Technical Drafting, Welding, and Welding Fabrication. SkillsUSA works directly with high schools and colleges, so ask your school counselor or teacher if it is an option for you.

- **Skills Compétences Canada** (http://skillscompetencescanada.com/en/skills-canada-national-competition). This nonprofit organization seeks to encourage Canadian youth to pursue careers in the skilled trades and technology sectors. Its National Competition allows young people to participate in more than forty skilled trade and technology competitions. As with SkillsUSA, there are no specific roofing competitions, but many contests in other areas that would be worthwhile for an aspiring roofer. Competitions include those in carpentry, brick masonry, sheet metal work, welding, other trades, and workplace safety. In addition to participating in the competitions, student attendees can check out a dedicated "Career Zone" that features exhibitors and participate in Try-A-Trade® and technology activities.

■ *View highlights from a recent SkillsUSA competition and learn about the benefits of participating in such an event:*

Build Something! You can't build or repair a roof on a house or factory yet, but you can experiment by building models of homes or buildings, complete with mini versions of roofs that use real building materials such as shingles or tiles. This will give you an idea of the various aspects a roofer needs to keep in mind as he or she builds the roof. After you try out a model, you can move on to building a small clubhouse or shed in your backyard, or maybe even a tree house. Experiment with various types of roofing materials to get a basic idea of what it's like to construct a roof. Ask your parents for help on these projects. The following books offer some good ideas:

- *Keep Out!: Build Your Own Backyard Clubhouse: A Step-by-Step Guide*, by Lee Mothes (Storey Publishing, LLC, 2013).

- *Microshelters: 59 Creative Cabins, Tiny Houses, Tree Houses, and Other Small Structures*, by Derek Diedricksen (Storey Publishing, LLC, 2015).

- *Backyard Treehouses: Building Plans, Tips, and Advice*, by Dan Wright (Lyons Press, 2018).

Sources of Additional Exploration

Contact the following organizations for more information on education and careers in the roofing industry:

Asphalt Roofing Manufacturers Association
https://asphaltroofing.org

Associated General Contractors of America
https://www.agc.org

Canadian Roofing Contractors' Association
https://roofingcanada.com

Metal Roofing and Cladding Association of Australia
http://www.mrcaa.com.au

National Federation of Roofing Contractors Limited
https://www.nfrc.co.uk

National Roofing Contractors Association
http://www.nrca.net

National Women in Roofing
http://www.nationalwomeninroofing.org

Roofing Industry Alliance for Progress
http://www.roofingindustryalliance.net

Roofing Tile Association of Australia
http://www.rtaa.com.au

United Union of Roofers, Waterproofers & Allied Workers
http://www.unionroofers.com

Participate in an Information Interview with a Roofer. In an information interview, you come armed with questions, not your resume or a request for a job. Your goal is to ask questions that will help you learn more about what roofers do, what they like and dislike about their job, and other questions that will help you find out if this career is a good option for you, or a better fit for someone else. You'll find that most roofers love discussing their careers. Here are some questions to ask during the interview:

- Can you tell me about a day in your life on the job?
- What's your work environment like? Do you have to travel for your job?
- What are the most challenging tools to use?
- What are the most important personal and professional qualities for people in your career?
- What's your favorite task on the job? Least favorite?
- What do you do to keep yourself safe on the job?
- What is the future employment outlook for roofers? How is the field changing?
- What can I do now to prepare for the field (classes, activities, projects, etc.)?
- What do you think is the best educational path to becoming a roofer?

Your school counselor, construction club teacher-mentor, or shop teacher can help arrange an information interview. Roofing unions and professional associations are good resources for this type of opportunity. You might also consider reaching out to a roofer on LinkedIn or asking your parents if they know any roofers who are willing to be interviewed.

Text-Dependent Questions

1. Why must roofers be good at troubleshooting?

2. What happens during a tour of a construction site?

3. What is an information interview? What questions should you ask during such an interview?

Research Project

Learn as much as you can about the various types of roofs and roofing materials. Write a report that details your findings.

■ *The hard work of roofers keeps us protected from the elements.*

Words to Understand

Baby Boomer: A person who was born from the early-to-mid 1940s through 1964.

economy: Activities related to production, consumption, and trade of services and goods in a city, state, region, or country.

Great Recession: A period of significant economic decline worldwide, beginning in December 2007 and ending in June 2009, in which many banks failed, the real estate sector crashed, trade declined, and many people lost their jobs.

organic compound adhesives: Components found in some adhesive and sealant products that react with nitrogen oxides in the air and sunlight to create a gas called ozone, which can create smog in the lower atmosphere and cause respiratory problems.

CHAPTER 6

The Future of the Roofing Occupation

The Big Picture

Where would we be without roofs? Well, we'd be wet, cold, and covered with snow, or have a very bad sunburn depending on the season. So, it's obvious that we need skilled roofers to repair existing roofs and build new ones.

But despite the steady need for roofers, there is an ongoing shortage of skilled workers. "Finding qualified workers" was cited as the number one concern of roofing industry professionals surveyed for *Roofing Contractor's* "2017 Commercial Roofing Trends" report. Ninety percent of respondents believed it was a major concern.

Globally, workers in the skilled trades were cited by employers as the most in-demand career field, according to the human resource consulting firm ManpowerGroup. By continent or region, skilled trades workers topped the most in-demand list in the Americas, Europe, the Middle East, and Africa. They ranked fourth in the Asia-Pacific region.

■ *There is a shortage of roofers in Canada.*

There are several reasons for the shortage. First, the world's population is growing and more homes and other buildings are being constructed, but there are not enough people entering the construction industry. Second, many **Baby Boomer** roofers are expected to retire in the next decade, and not enough young people are pursuing careers in roofing to replace them. The idea that you need a bachelor's degree to get a good job has been drummed into the minds of many young people. But this is untrue. While earning a bachelor's degree in a high-demand field is certainly a worthwhile choice, many trades careers provide a stable middle-class lifestyle. ("Middle-class" is an economic category that includes 25 percent to 65 percent of households in the United States, Canada, and other countries.) Other young people believe stereotypes about the trades: that they're only for dumb people who couldn't make it in college, that they're too messy and physically demanding, and they do not pay well. But the facts don't support these beliefs. Roofing systems have grown increasingly complex—especially with the growing use of solar photovoltaic systems and energy efficient building materials and construction techniques. Roofers certainly use their muscles and get dirty on the job. But they also use their analytical, troubleshooting, and, if they own a company, their business skills. Finally, while entry-level roofers don't make stellar salaries, roofing contractors with successful businesses can earn $90,000 to $200,000 or more, depending on the size of their companies. "Dumb" people don't earn that amount of money.

But back to global demand for roofers. The recruitment firm Michael Page recently conducted research to determine demand for specific careers by country. It found that there is a shortage of roofers in Canada, Australia, Sweden, and Austria.

Demand for roofers is also strong in the United States. Job opportunities are expected to increase by 11 percent during the next decade, according to the U.S. Department of Labor. This is faster than the average growth (7 percent) predicted for all careers. There will be many new jobs for roofers because of the following factors:

- Many roofers are nearing retirement age, and there are currently not enough people entering the field to replace those who are retiring.

- Many people leave the field because it is too physically demanding and pay for entry-level roofers is not as good as the pay is for entry-level workers in other trades.

- There has been a strong increase in new residential and commercial construction since the **Great Recession**, and demand has increased for roofers. Job opportunities for roofers in the construction industry are expected to grow by 14 percent during the next decade—much faster than the average for all careers.

- The roofing industry is less affected by economic downturns than other sectors. Although the number of new buildings that are constructed will decline during a recession, there will be a steady need for roofers to repair or replace existing roofs because all roofs eventually wear out and need to be repaired or replaced.

- The alternative energy (especially solar and wind) sector is enjoying strong growth, and demand is growing for roofers who are skilled in the installation of photovoltaic panels and tiles, wind turbines, and related components on roofs. Tesla recently launched Solar Roof, roofing tiles that convert sunlight into electricity. Roofers who are knowledgeable regarding the installation and repair of the photovoltaic tiles will be in strong demand.

- Roofers will be needed to repair or replace roofs after hurricanes, tornadoes, massive wildfires, earthquakes, and other natural disasters. One example of the massive destruction to homes caused by natural disasters is Hurricane Harvey, which, as of September 5, 2017, had damaged 203,000 homes, of which 12,700 were destroyed. That's a lot of roofs that need repair or replacement.

■ *Natural disasters, such as the tornado that damaged this roof, create steady work for roofers.*

■ *Learn more about Tesla's Solar Roof:*

New Technologies

Technology is steadily changing everything from how apprentice roofers train for the job, to the tools roofers use, the types of building materials that are used to construct roofs, and much more.

Apprentices now receive some of their training via computer simulations and smart boards. They review blueprints and diagrams on tablet computers, and are trained in how to use the latest digital tools.

On the job, roofers still use hammers, nail guns, and chalk lines, but they also use digital devices such as thermal imaging scanners, moisture meters, and roofing energy calculators (which can provide customers with information on the energy savings offered by different roofing systems and other useful data). Other major technological innovations include:

- Roofing design simulators, which allow contractors to show customers how a roof will look before it is installed on their home

- Drones, cameras, and video cameras, which are used to document the condition of the roof before and after the work is done, and to reduce the amount of time roofers spend on a roof

- Green roofing technologies, including solar roofs, energy-efficient roof membranes, and low– or zero–volatile **organic compound adhesives**

■ *Drones allow roofing contractors to safely assess the condition of a roof before having to physically inspect the structure.*

Business owners use office and customer management software, the internet and social media to market their businesses and communicate with customers and coworkers, and building information modeling software, a computer application that uses a 3-D model-based process to more efficiently plan, design, build, and manage buildings and infrastructure.

The roofing industry is changing rapidly due to these and other technologies. Roofers need to stay up-to-date with technology to stay competitive.

Challenges to Employment Growth

Demand is high for roofers, but in the future, a few developments may bring employment growth back to earth. If the **economy** takes a hit, the number of new construction projects will decline, and job opportunities for roofers will slow. Of course, there will still be a need for roofers to repair or replace existing roofs, but, regardless, there will be fewer jobs. Additionally, breakthroughs in roofing materials

Women in the Roofing Industry

Women make up about 47 percent of the U.S. workforce, but only 2 to 10 percent of roofing industry professionals. And many of these female roofing professionals work in management, clerical, sales, or public relations positions. The roofing industry is trying to encourage young women to enter this field by hosting open houses and networking events, establishing mentorship programs, and offering other programs and resources. Here are some organizations that provide support to women in roofing and the construction industry:

- National Women in Roofing (http://nationalwomeninroofing. org) seeks to recruit women into the roofing industry. It offers networking events, a mentoring program, and educational resources for women.

- The United Union of Roofers, Waterproofers & Allied Workers (http://www.unionroofers.com) actively seeks to increase the number of women in the roofing industry.

- The Women's Bureau of the U.S. Department of Labor provides information on organizations and programs that seek to increase the number of women in the construction, protection services, and transportation industries at its website, https:// www.dol.gov/wb/NTO/workers/apprenticeships.

- The National Association of Women in Construction (NAWIC, http://www.nawic.org) offers membership, an annual meeting, and scholarships. It also publishes The NAWIC IMAGE.

- The Canadian Association of Women in Construction (http:// www.cawic.ca) offers membership, a mentoring networking events, and a job bank at its website.

and construction methods may increase the lifespan of roofs so that they only need to be replaced every fifty to seventy years (instead of twenty to thirty years). This development would also reduce demand for roofers. Finally, if more people decide to become roofers, the current shortage of roofers will evaporate and it will be harder to find jobs. But even if demand slows in one part of a country, or an entire country, a roofer can relocate to an area where demand is better.

■ *There are many opportunities for women in the roofing industry.*

In Closing

Can you see yourself atop a home putting the finishing touches on a new roof? Do you like working with both your hands and head to solve problems and help others? Are you looking for a career that offers competitive pay and many jobs without a four-year degree? If so, then a career as a roofer could be in your future. I hope that you'll use this book as a starting point to discover even more about a career as a roofer. Talk to roofers about their careers and shadow them on the job, interview roofing contractors to learn about the rewards and challenges of being a business owner, use the resources of professional organizations and unions, and try out some projects (build a backyard clubhouse with a cool roof that you design, for example) to hone your skills. Good luck on your career exploration!

■ *Opportunities in roofing are excellent for creative problem-solvers who don't mind working hard and enjoy working outdoors.*

Did You Know?

- About 116,000 roofers are employed in the United States. Ninety-one percent work for foundation, structure, and building exterior contractors.
- Approximately 21 percent of roofers are self-employed.
- About 9 percent of workers in the construction industry are women.

Source: U.S. Department of Labor

Text-Dependent Questions

1. Why is employment strong for roofers?

2. What are some organizations that support women roofers?

3. What are some developments that might slow employment for roofers?

Research Project

Learn more about Tesla's Solar Roof by visiting https://www.tesla.com/solarroof. Write a report about the benefits and drawbacks of using this type of product and present it to your class.

apprentice: A trainee who is enrolled in a program that prepares them to work as a skilled trades worker. Apprentices must complete 2,000 hours of on-the-job training and 144 hours of related classroom instruction during a four- to five-year course of study. They are paid a salary that increases as they obtain experience.

apprenticeship: A formal training program that often consists of 2,000 hours of on-the-job training and 144 hours of related classroom instruction per year for four to five years.

bid: A formal offer created by a contractor or trades worker that details the work that will be done, the amount the company or individual will charge, and the time frame in which the work will be completed.

blueprints: A reproduction of a technical plan for the construction of a home or other structure. Blueprints are created by licensed architects.

building codes: A series of rules established by local, state, regional, and national governments that ensure safe construction. The National Electrical Code, which was developed by the National Fire Protection Association, is an example of a building code in the United States.

building information modeling software: A computer application that uses a 3D model-based process that helps construction, architecture, and engineering professionals to more efficiently plan, design, build, and manage buildings and infra-structure.

building materials: Any naturally-occurring (clay, rocks, sand, wood, etc.) or human-made substances (steel, cement, etc.) that are used to construct buildings and other structures.

building permit: Written permission from a government entity that allows trades workers to construct, alter, or otherwise work at a construction site.

community college: A private or public two-year college that awards certificates and associate degrees.

general contractor: A licensed individual or company that accepts primary responsibility for work done at a construction site or in another setting.

green construction: The planning, design, construction, and operation of structures in an environmentally responsible manner. Green construction stresses energy and water efficiency, the use of eco-friendly construction materials (when possible), indoor environmental quality, and the structure's overall effects on its site or the larger community. Also known as **green building**.

inspection: The process of reviewing/examining ongoing or recently completed construction work to ensure that it has been completed per the applicable building codes. Construction and building inspectors are employed by government agencies and private companies that provide inspection services to potential purchasers of new construction or remodeled buildings.

job foreman: A journeyman (male or female) who manages a group of other journeymen and apprentices on a project.

journeyman: A trades worker who has completed an apprenticeship training. If licensed, he or she can work without direct supervision, but, for large projects, must work under permits issued to a master electrician.

Leadership in Energy and Environmental Design (LEED) certification: A third-party verification that remodeled or newly constructed buildings have met the highest criteria for water efficiency, energy efficiency, the use of eco-friendly materials and building practices, indoor environmental quality, and other criteria. LEED certification is the most popular green building rating system in the world.

master trades worker: A trades professional who has a minimum level of experience (usually at least three to four years as a licensed professional) and who has passed an examination. Master trades workers manage journeymen, trades workers, and apprentices.

prefabricated: The manufacture or fabrication of certain components of a structure (walls, electrical components, etc.) away from the construction site. Prefabricated products are brought to the construction site and joined with existing structures or components.

schematic diagram: An illustration of the components of a system that uses abstract, graphic symbols instead of realistic pictures or illustrations.

self-employment: Working for oneself as a small business owner, rather than for a corporation or other employer. Self-employed people are responsible for generating their own income, and they must provide their own fringe benefits (such as health insurance).

smart home technology: A system of interconnected devices that perform certain actions to save energy, time, and money.

technical college: A public or private college that offers two- or four-year programs in practical subjects, such as the trades, information technology, applied sciences, agriculture, and engineering.

union: An organization that seeks to gain better wages, benefits, and working conditions for its members. Also called a **labor union** or **trade union**.

zoning permit: A document issued by a government body that stipulates that the project in question meets existing zoning rules for a geographic area.

zoning rules: Restrictions established by government bodies as to what type of structure can be built in a certain area. For example, many cities have zoning rules that restrict the construction of factories in residential areas.

Index

Photo Credits

Cover: Monkey Business Images | Dreamstime.com

Interior book cover: Manon Ringuette | Dreamstime.com

7: Olha Hutsuliuk | Dreamstime.com

9: Bambulla | Dreamstime.com

10: Andrii Zhezhera | Dreamstime.com

11: Sebastian Czapnik | Dreamstime.com

14: Oleksandr Rado | Dreamstime.com

15: Stockage | Dreamstime.com

17: Dean Hammel | Dreamstime.com

19: Zoransimin | Dreamstime.com

22: Awcnz62 | Dreamstime.com

24–25: Tonny Wu | Dreamstime

24: Peter Lewis | Dreamstime.com

24: Nathan King | Dreamstime.com

24: Oleg63sam | Dreamstime.com

26: Hamik | Dreamstime.com

29: Mira Agron | Dreamstime

29: Solarium | Dreamstime.com

29: Wisconsinart | Dreamstime.com

31: Lowerkase | Dreamstime.com

31: Dmitry Kalinovsky | Dreamstime.com

32: Auremar | Dreamstime.com

33: Marek Uliasz | Dreamstime.com

35: Auremar | Dreamstime.com

36: Auremar | Dreamstime.com

38: Katarzyna Bialasiewicz | Dreamstime.com

42: Viacheslav Iacobchuk | Dreamstime.com

45: Monkey Business Images | Dreamstime.com

50: Calvin Leake | Dreamstime.com

51: Dpproductions | Dreamstime.com

52: Sculpies | Dreamstime.com

54: Monkey Business Images | Dreamstime.com

56: Ronnie Wu | Dreamstime.com

57: Monkey Business Images | Dreamstime.com

62: Brenda Carson | Dreamstime.com

63: Lilith76 | Dreamstime.com

65: Laura Ballard | Dreamstime.com

67: Dmitry Kalinovsky | Dreamstime.com

69: Pojoslaw | Dreamstime.com

70: Sculpies | Dreamstime.com

Further Reading & Internet Resources

Addis, Bill. *Building: 3,000 Years of Design, Engineering, and Construction*. New York: Phaidon Press, 2015.

Editors of Fine Homebuilding. *Siding, Roofing*, and Trim. Newtown, Conn.: The Taunton Press, 2014.

Mindham, C. N. *Goss's Roofing Ready Reckoner: From Timberwork to Tiles*. 5th ed. Hoboken, N.J.: Wiley-Blackwell, 2016.

Internet Resources

https://www.bls.gov/ooh/construction-and-extraction/roofers.htm#tab-1: This article from the *Occupational Outlook Handbook* provides information on job duties, educational requirements, salaries, and the employment outlook for roofers.

http://www.byf.org: This web initiative of the National Center for Construction Education and Research offers overviews of more than thirty careers in the trades (including roofers), videos of trades workers on the job, and much more.

http://www.careersinconstruction.ca/en/career/roofershingler: This website from BuildForce Canada provides information on job duties, training, and salaries for roofers.

https://nationalcareersservice.direct.gov.uk/job-profiles/roofer: This resource from the United Kingdom's National Careers Service provides information on job duties, educational requirements, key skills, salaries, and the work environment for roofers.

https://www.careerfaqs.com.au/careers/how-to-become-a-roofer-in-australia-careers-in-construction: This website provides an overview of how to become a roofer in Australia.

About the Author

Andrew Morkes has been a writer and editor for more than 25 years. He is the author of more than 20 books about college-planning and careers, including many titles in this series, the *Vault Career Guide to Social Media*, and *They Teach That in College!?: A Resource Guide to More Than 100 Interesting College Majors*, which was selected as one of the best books of the year by the library journal *Voice of Youth Advocates*. He is also the author and publisher of "The Morkes Report: College and Career Planning Trends" blog.

Video Credits

Chapter 1: Learn more about the rewards of working as a roofer: http://x-qr.net/1Fck

Learn about the work environment for roofers, the rewards of working in the field, and opportunities for advancement into roofing design and engineering: http://x-qr.net/1Fh9

Learn more about the importance of wearing safety gear when working on a roof: http://x-qr.net/1H5d

Chapter 4: Learn more about the many benefits of participating in a roofing apprenticeship: http://x-qr.net/1F2a

Learn how a roofing apprentice developed social skills during his apprenticeship: http://x-qr.net/1EhR

Chapter 5: Get some hands-on experience by learning how to use a chalk line: http://x-qr.net/1Ec6

View highlights from a recent SkillsUSA competition and learn about the benefits of participating in such an event: http://x-qr.net/1EYz

Chapter 6: Learn more about Tesla's Solar Roof: http://x-qr.net/1Hho